CARL LAFERTOI

THE REAL
EASTER

The Real Easter (3rd Edition)
Copyright © 2017 Christianity Explored.
Reprinted 2017, 2018 (twice), 2018, 2020, 2022.

Published by:
The Good Book Company

thegoodbook.com | thegoodbook.co.uk
thegoodbook.com.au | thegoodbook.co.nz | thegoodbook.co.in

Unless otherwise indicated, Scripture is taken from the HOLY BIBLE, NEW INTERNATIONAL VERSION. Copyright © 1978, 1984 International Bible Society.

Used by permission of Zondervan Bible Publishers.

All rights reserved. Except as may be permitted by the Copyright Act, no portion of this publication may be reproduced in any form or by any means without prior permission from the publisher.

Design by André Parker

ISBN: 9781784982638 | Printed in Turkey

THE REAL
EASTER

It was a mistake that cost them millions. On New Year's Day 1962, a group of scruffy lads with guitars recorded a demo tape and gave it to Dick Rowe, a producer at Decca Records. Decca rejected it, reputedly telling them, "Guitar bands are on their way out". This band of hopefuls were an outdated irrelevance in the 1960s, Decca decided.

George Martin, a producer at EMI, reacted very differently to the boys, who called themselves *The Beatles*. As soon as he heard their raw sound he signed them up. Within two years, John, Paul, George and Ringo had multiple chart-busting hits in the UK and America; Beatlemania swept the world. Martin found himself part of the biggest music story of all time.

Since then, one billion Beatles records have been sold worldwide. Maybe guitar groups weren't on their way out after all! Decca's decision cost them millions: EMI's decision made them millions.

One day; two reactions; two very different outcomes.

This story of reactions and decisions could be repeated a million times over. At a sports match, one chief scout sees a star; another sees only a donkey. At a fashion show, one designer spots genius; others see only a mess. Time alone tells who is right.

All events are like that. And it's exactly the same with the events of Easter. Not the eggs-and-bunny-rabbit version of Easter, but the real Easter – the first Good Friday and Easter Sunday almost 2,000 years ago.

Not such a Good Friday

That Friday, which came to be called "Good", was anything but good for three particular men. Sentenced to be executed in one of the most brutal ways ever invented by mankind, these three were whipped and then forced to carry their own cross to the place where they would die in agony hours later. On a hilltop outside Jerusalem they were nailed through their hands and feet and then lifted up high to be mocked by the crowd.

Three crosses. Three men. Hanging in a row.

The two men on either side were criminals, terrorists. They were guilty of terrible crimes and were paying for their actions. *But the man in the middle was different.*

He had been the leader of a new movement which claimed to have the answers to the big questions of life.

THE REAL EASTER

He claimed to know the way to live life as it was meant to be lived. He claimed to be the way to God. His name was Jesus; he came from a small town in northern Israel called Nazareth. He said he was God's all-powerful King, his "Christ". To the shock and astonishment of his countrymen, he claimed to be God's own Son – God himself walking round in a human skin.

As they nailed him to a criminal's cross, he looked nothing of the sort. He had already endured hours of beating, mockery and torture. The Roman soldiers who carried out the execution had stripped him, and placed a sneering sign above his head: "The King of the Jews".

A man called Luke, who carefully researched the events of that day with people who were actually there, records what happened next:

> *The people stood watching, and the rulers even sneered at him. They said, "He saved others; let him save himself if he is the Christ of God, the Chosen One." The soldiers also came up and mocked him. They offered him wine vinegar and said, "If you are the king of the Jews, save yourself." ... One of the criminals who hung there hurled insults at him: "Aren't you the Christ? Save yourself and us!"*

Luke 23 v 35-39

Most people there that day reacted in the same way to this Jesus as he hung dying on his cross. They saw a failure, a fake. They thought it impossible that this crucified man could be a King. Even one of the criminals found the breath to shout insults at him.

Another view

But Luke's account doesn't end there—because one man reacted very differently to what was going on.

> *The other criminal rebuked him [the first criminal]. "Don't you fear God," he said, "since you are under the same sentence? We are punished justly, for we are getting what our deeds deserve. But this man has done nothing wrong." Then he said, "Jesus, remember me when you come into your kingdom."*
>
> Luke 23 v 40-42

Here's an alternative view of the same death, the same event. This second criminal was dying, and he knew that he deserved to die: "We are getting what our deeds deserve". But as he looked at Jesus dying next to him, he understood that "this man has done nothing wrong". He realized that Jesus was not like him. He deserved to die – Jesus didn't.

And this criminal had decided something else too. He'd decided that the sign above Jesus' head, which mocked him for his claims to be a King, was actually, ironically, spot on. He recognized Jesus was a King, and he thought that the place Jesus would rule over was a place beyond death. When he looked at Jesus he saw the future.

So he asked the bleeding, dying man next to him to "remember me when you come into your kingdom".

And Jesus' answer is one which has changed thousands of lives, and deaths, ever since:

> *"I tell you the truth, today you will be with me in paradise."* Luke 23 v 43

One day – Good Friday. Two reactions – rejecting Jesus as irrelevant, or recognizing King Jesus as the future. And, according to Jesus, two very different outcomes.

The man on one side died as he deserved; the man on the other had a place in paradise he did not deserve. As one man faced the end, leaving behind everything he'd ever had, the other found a new beginning, leaving behind all the mistakes he'd ever made. He could look forward to a wonderful life beyond his own death.

One day; two reactions; two very different outcomes.

Promises kept

But, of course, Jesus was just a defeated man dying on a cross. How could anyone trust a word he said?

After all, here was a man who'd promised he was the

CHRISTIANITY EXPLORED

way to get to heaven; and who'd promised he would come back to life after dying. But he was buried like everyone else, his friends and family grieved as all bereaved families do, and everyone else went back to normal as people always do.

Until three days later – when Jesus' tomb was found empty.

That was strange enough, but then that same morning Jesus appeared to a friend of his, Mary. And that afternoon he walked along with a couple of men who'd known him before his death. In the evening, he ate dinner with a dozen of his closest friends, and then a few weeks later was seen by five hundred people at the same time. There was no doubt about it: Jesus was alive. The claims he'd made about himself were true.

He was God's King.

The greatest mistake in life

It's easy when we hear about that far-off day when Jesus died to think of ourselves as onlookers, passers-by. But we're not. Our place in the events of Good Friday is the place of those two criminals.

That sounds outrageous! But just as they were both facing death, so are we. We may not die on a cross but we will each die one day; it's the only certain fact of your life. And just as that pair deserved to experience death, so do we. Just as those criminals had chosen to

THE REAL EASTER

risk ignoring their rulers, so have we. And the Ruler we ignore is God.

We live in the world he's created; we enjoy the bodies he's made for us; we take the gifts of health, wealth, love and happiness that he offers us. And then we choose to live our lives our way, making up the rules for ourselves instead of living by his, deciding to make ourselves kings instead of accepting that he is in charge.

People reject God in different ways. Some reject him by doing awful things. Others are really quite nice, respectable people. Curiously, many people even reject God while following a religion. But we all naturally ignore God and break his rules. I do it; you do it; we all do it. The Bible puts it this way: "All have sinned and fall short of the glory of God" (Romans 3:23).

If we look hard enough, we can see the effects our sin has on our relationships with the people around us. We've all been confronted by the tearful eyes or the broken heart that we've caused. However good we like to think we are, there are things we've said and done that we regret.

But what we can't see, yet, is the effect that our sin has on our relationship with God.

A few years ago, I decided to ignore the "50" signs in some major roadworks. Despite the narrow lanes, my foot pressed down until the needle crept up to 70. My friend in the passenger seat was annoyed that I was speeding; my relationship with them was affected. But what I didn't know at the time was that my relationship with the police had also been affected. It was only a month later that the full cost of my actions became clear when a letter came through the door. I had broken the law in this country, and I had been caught. Now I faced prosecution, instead of protection, from the police. I was fined and had points added to my licence.

Our sin changes our relationship with God. It prevents us from being his friends and makes us his enemies. And just as there's a punishment for breaking the law, so there's a consequence for ignoring God and his rules in his world. If we continue to ignore God, then we will eventually lose all the good things that God gives us: happiness, friendship, love, life, everything. The punishment for sin is spiritual death, an eternity outside God's perfect kingdom.

However great life may seem right now, continuing to rebel against God is the greatest mistake any of us can ever make. In the end it will cost us everything.

A divine swap

The story is told of a Native American tribe whose chickens were being stolen. The chief announced that when caught, the criminal would be whipped as the deserved punishment for breaking the law in his tribe.

One day there was a commotion in the camp in

the dead of night and the chief was summoned. The chicken-stealer had been caught. To the chief's horror, it was his son.

Justice had to be done – the son had to be punished. But just as the son was about to be whipped, the chief got off his chair, ran to him and wrapped himself around his back.

The whip fell on the chief instead of the son. The chief took the punishment instead of his son.

God could have left you and me to suffer his punishment and experience the eternity without him that we've chosen. But because he loves the people he's made, he didn't. God's Son came to earth as a man, as Jesus Christ. And he came not to live in luxury or rule from a throne but to die on that cross. His purpose in living in his world was to die in it on that first "Good" Friday.

Why? One of his best friends, Peter, explained that "Christ died for sins once for all, the righteous for the unrighteous, to bring you to God" (1 Peter 3:18).

As that second criminal recognised, it was God's King dying on the cross. As this dying criminal understood, we – the unrighteous – deserve death, but Christ – the righteous – didn't. And yet Christ died for the unrighteous, suffering the agony of death instead of those who deserved it. When Jesus died, he took upon himself the punishment of separation from his Father –

so that we don't have to.

On the cross God took the penalty for our rebellion upon himself and died our death.

Two reactions; two futures

So we find ourselves in the same position as those criminals, facing a spiritual death that we all deserve. And we will react to Jesus' death in one of the two ways they did.

We can look at Christ's cross and see an irrelevance, a historical detail. We may politely ignore him or even laugh at the idea that this man is God's King. We can live our lives our way, by our rules, putting ourselves first.

Life in God's world, living however we want, can look and feel fantastic; but ultimately it's the greatest mistake we can make. It will only lead to spiritual death: an eternity separated from God's love, from his goodness and his gifts.

But there's a second way.

The other criminal looked at Christ's cross and saw a different future – and you can too. You can decide not to reject God's King, but to ask him to change your eternal future.

You can recognize that the Jesus who rose from the dead really is God's Son. You can accept that your rebellion against God, your rightful Ruler, leaves you deserving spiritual death. And you can ask Jesus to give you a fresh start with God now, and a new life that lasts forever. Because he died in your place, you can be forgiven. Because he rose again, he can give you new life. And because he is merciful and loves you, he longs to give you these gifts today.

One day – Jesus' death on the cross. Two reactions – rejection or recognition. Two outcomes – eternal death or eternal life.

Why make a mistake that will cost you everything? Why not recognize that the Jesus who rose from the dead really is the Christ? Why not ask the Christ – who died so you don't have to – to give you an undeserved place in his eternal kingdom?

Why not hear the crucified Christ Jesus say to you, *I tell you the truth, when you die you'll be with me in paradise*?

One day. Two reactions. Two outcomes. One vital decision. Yours…

What next?

Talk to God. If you want to start a new life following Jesus Christ as your King, you could use the words below to mark the beginning of your Christian life. He is waiting to hear from you, and would love to forgive you and give you eternal life.

> *Jesus, I recognize that you are God's Son and God's King.*
> *I know that I haven't lived with you as my King.*
> *I know I don't deserve a place in your eternal kingdom.*
> *Thank you for dying on the cross to take the punishment I deserve.*
> *Thank you for rising again to give me new life.*
> *Please forgive me, come and live in me by your Spirit, and give me a fresh start with God.*
> *From now on, please help me to live in your world with you as my Ruler. Amen*

If you've said those words to Jesus Christ, you've started an amazing new eternal life! It's a good idea to tell another Christian about it, so that they can offer you support.

Join a Course. If you still have questions, why not join a *Christianity Explored* or *Life Explored* course? It's informal and relaxed. You won't be asked to read aloud, pray or sing. You can ask any question you like – or you can just sit and listen. Visit www.christianityexplored.org, click "What's Next", and scroll down to "Find a Church or Course Near You".

Read a Book. A great one to start with is *One life. What's it all about?* Get a copy at thegoodbook.co.uk/one life or thegoodbook.com/onelife.

THE REAL EASTER

- One day...
- One death...
- Two reactions...
- Two outcomes...

What is the real Easter all about?